IMAGES
of Rail

The SOUTHERN RAILWAY

FURTHER RECOLLECTIONS

Locomotive No. 750 is shown in front of the Southern Railway Office Building in this 1970 photograph. To the left of the bridge is the Atlanta Terminal Station. (Martin K. O'Toole.)

IMAGES
of Rail

The SOUTHERN
RAILWAY
FURTHER RECOLLECTIONS

C. Pat Cates, Dick Hillman, and Sallie Loy
for the Southern Museum of Civil War
and Locomotive History
and the Southern Railway Historical Association

ARCADIA
PUBLISHING

Copyright © 2005 by the Kennesaw Museum Foundation, Inc.
ISBN 978-1-5316-1244-3

Published by Arcadia Publishing
Charleston, South Carolina

Library of Congress Catalog Card Number: 2005923387

For all general information contact Arcadia Publishing at:
Telephone 843-853-2070
Fax 843-853-0044
E-mail sales@arcadiapublishing.com
For customer service and orders:
Toll-Free 1-888-313-2665

Visit us on the Internet at www.arcadiapublishing.com

Locomotive No. 6143, a 1950 FP7, passes an excursion train near Gainesville, Georgia, in this 1970 photograph. (Martin K. O'Toole.)

CONTENTS

Introduction   7

1. Facilities of the Southern Railway   9

2. Passenger Trains and Equipment   45

3. The Southern Railway Goes to War   59

4. Working on the Railroad   89

5. Steam Trains on the Southern Railway   103

Acknowledgments   127

Bibliography   128

Locomotive No. 4501 is pictured near Dayton, Tennessee, in October 1969. (Martin K. O'Toole.)

INTRODUCTION

The history of the Southern Railway has its roots in the South Carolina Canal and Railroad Company, which was chartered in 1827 and operated its first train, the *Best Friend of Charleston*, in 1830. The Southern Railway grew to become a rail system that was spread over thousands of miles across the southeastern United States. In 1982, the Southern Railway was merged with the Norfolk and Western Railway Company and is known today as the Norfolk Southern Railway Company.

Our first book, *Images of Rail: The Southern Railway*, gave an overview of the railroad and showed a sampling of its many facets. In this volume, we will give the reader a closer look at a number of subjects, including Inman and John Sevier Yards and the Spencer Shops in North Carolina. In addition, the evolution of passenger service will be examined, and the history of the Southern Steam Excursion Program will be documented through interviews with its major participants. People are the most important facet of any railroad, and this book will look at a variety of occupations, as well as the railroaders who served their country during World War II.

Rail Yards play a significant role in the operation of a railroad. Among the numerous yards of the Southern Railway are Inman Yard, located in Atlanta, Georgia, and John Sevier Yard in Knoxville, Tennessee. These yards were initially constructed in the early 20th century and were modernized in the 1950s. Dramatic photographs illustrate how these yards were improved to keep pace with the growing Southern Railway. The rail yard in Spencer, North Carolina, was also an important yard, which was located next to the historic Spencer Shops. Spencer Shops were constructed in 1896 to provide a repair facility for the Southern Railway, which had only been in existence for two years. This well known facility was an important shop in the transitional period from steam to diesel locomotives. Today it is the site of the North Carolina Transportation Museum.

Passenger trains played an enormous role in the development of the United States. Until their advent in the 1840s, the transportation system in this country was limited to horses and boats. Although crude at their inception, passenger trains developed over the years into a comfortable and sophisticated way to travel. The history of the passenger service on the Southern Railway will be explored using vintage pictures depicting the earliest passenger equipment to modern photographs highlighting the continuation of one of the most famous Southern passenger trains, the *Crescent*, by Amtrak.

During times of war, railroads have been critical in getting supplies and manpower to the locations where they are needed. The story of military railroads dates to the Civil War. Contained within the walls of the Southern Museum of Civil War and Locomotive History is the famous locomotive, the *General*, which was captured in Big Shanty, Georgia, by a group of Yankee soldiers disguised as civilians. Desperate to destroy an important Southern railroad, their attempt was thwarted by the determination of a handful of Southerners. Also contained in the museum is the story of the 727th Railway Operating Battalion in World War II. This little-known story recounts the battalion that was trained and sponsored by the Southern Railway during a critical time in the history of this country. The soldiers of this battalion served in most of the operations in the European theater and were cited by Gen. George S. Patton for their accomplishments on the island of Sicily.

Jim Bistline, retired general counsel and general manager, steam operations, of the Southern Railway, commented that telling the story of the people that worked for the Southern Railway was one of the best ways to capture the spirit that made the railroad such a great company. Many of the businesses familiar to the casual observer are confined within the walls of an office building or factory. Such is not the case with a railroad that has its facilities and personnel scattered over a wide area. Railroad people have to be possessed with great self-reliance and dedication to work, sometimes in difficult situations, without a great deal of direct supervision. The workers of the railroad take care of many people and millions of dollars of equipment, and it is to their dedication that we highlight some of the diverse jobs they perform.

Steam-powered equipment has long held a great fascination for people. When diesel locomotives replaced steam in the 1950s, the opportunities to experience these fascinating machines began to rapidly decline. Almost 40 years ago, the Southern Railway made a corporate decision to run special passenger trains powered by steam locomotives. The Southern Railway was determined to preserve the steam era through their Excursion Program, and the people loved it. From those who rode the trains to those who watched from the sidelines, the excitement of a steam-powered train thundering across the countryside has been captured in a wonderful collection of photographs. Also pictured will be the people that brought the program to life and sustained it throughout its colorful existence.

The Southern Railroad was vitally important to the growth and development of the southeastern United States. The early railroad connected seaports and river cities with the inland communities and agricultural centers and eventually grew into a web of thousands of miles of rail lines. Between 1830 and 1930, most of the freight and passenger service in this country moved by way of the railroad. While railroads are no longer the predominate means of moving passenger traffic, they continue to play a major role in the movement of freight.

The Southern Museum of Civil War and Locomotive History is grateful to the Southern Railway Historical Association for the job they have done in preserving the archives of this colorful company. It is a pleasure to continue the story of the Southern Railway through the use of archival photographs from their collection as well as a number of current photographs taken by a new breed of photographers. It is through the efforts of everyone working together that the history of the Southern Railway will continue to be enjoyed by countless generations.

One

FACILITIES OF THE
SOUTHERN RAILWAY

Soon after the Southern Railway came into operation in 1894, it found itself in need of an additional facility to make repairs to newly acquired equipment. Samuel Spencer, president of the company, realized that the facilities in Atlanta and Knoxville could not handle all the repair work and looked for a new location on the main line between Washington and Atlanta. In 1896, the Southern Railway purchased land in Rowan County, North Carolina. Soon workmen descended on farmland north of Salisbury, North Carolina, to begin construction of the new facility, which was named for Samuel Spencer. The resulting town that would flourish around the repair shops was also named Spencer. In addition to a roundhouse and numerous shops, there was also a freight yard and terminal facilities. An 0-6-0 switcher is shown here on duty at Spencer Yard. This photograph, taken in 1947, also shows a rear view of the Spencer Shops with the back shop featured prominently in the center. (David Driscoll).

The photographs on this page show two views of the roundhouse and turntable in 1947. In the mid-1920s, it was determined that the turntable and roundhouse being used were inadequate to service all the locomotives in the Southern fleet, and a new, 37-stall roundhouse and 100-foot roundtable were constructed. The roundhouse was named for Bob Julian, roundhouse supervisor. (David Driscoll.)

The Bob Julian Roundhouse was the only roundhouse in the Southern Railway System that was named for a person. In the late 1940s, the roundhouse underwent renovations to service diesel locomotives and continued operations until the 1970s, when the Southern Railway donated the land and buildings to the North Carolina Transportation Museum. (David Driscoll.)

This 1946 photograph shows the coaling tower. The 110-foot coal chute had been built in 1913 and became obsolete in 1953, when the last steam locomotive was retired. It was demolished in June of that same year. (David Driscoll.)

Both of these photographs were taken in the roundhouse during the 1940s. In the photograph to the left, workers perform repairs to locomotive No. 1575. The tool box of C. W. Waller is shown in the photograph above. (David Driscoll.)

As the Southern Railway grew, it purchased a variety of locomotives that required larger maintenance facilities. In 1904, construction began on a new building, which would serve as machine and erecting shops. When the building was completed in 1905, it was called "the back shop" by the employees, a name which it retains today. The photographs on this page show the interior of the back shop. (David Driscoll.)

The Southern Railway purchased its first diesel locomotives in 1941, and by 1953, it would be the first major railroad to completely scrap its fleet of steam locomotives. In this 1946 photograph, steam locomotives are being repaired in the back shop, while two diesel locomotives can be seen forward of the steam locomotives on the left. (David Driscoll.)

Diesel locomotive No. 4104 is in the back shop for repairs following an accident at Danville, Virginia. (David Driscoll.)

This diesel engine assembly line was located in the back shop. Engines identified for overhaul or repair were placed on dollies that rode over rails from one work station to the next, where they were systematically dismantled, reconditioned, and reassembled. Parts removed from the engines went to various sub-shops where they were cleaned, tested, and repaired. As the engines were repaired, they were returned to their starting point along a similar assembly line, where a powerful crane lifted them for installation in their respective locomotives.

This 1950 photograph shows diesels sandwiched between steam locomotives with the back shop in the background. Imagine the difficulty the workers must have faced as they serviced two entirely different kinds of machines in the same facility. (David Driscoll.)

A photograph of Spencer Yard shows a freight train moving through the yard while a diesel switcher awaits its next orders. Spencer Yard was one of the largest on the Southern Railway. In 1907, a transfer facility opened near the Spencer shops. Known as the "transfer sheds," the facility was vital for the distribution of carloads of goods to consumers throughout the South.

A unique photograph taken on April 13, 1953, at Spencer shops shows the *Best Friend of Charleston*, a diesel EMD-FT, and two steam locomotives, No. 544 and No. 1393.

In 1977, the Southern Railway donated four acres of land and three buildings to the State of North Carolina. A second donation in 1979 placed the entire area under the management of the Department of Cultural Resources. Today the North Carolina Transportation Museum is a showplace of railroad history made possible through the efforts of the museum staff and countless volunteers. (Dick Hillman.)

Spencer, North Carolina, is seen then and now. The photograph above was taken in 1940 of downtown Spencer showing the electrical substation and the Southern Railway tank behind it. The town of Spencer can be seen to the left. The substation building, tank, and town appeared relatively unchanged 61 years later. The photograph below, taken in 2001, shows an excursion train providing enjoyment to visitors at the North Carolina Transportation Museum. (Top photograph: David Driscoll; bottom photograph: Dick Hillman)

This photograph shows Knoxville, Tennessee, in 1882. The depot (at left) and the roundhouse (behind overpass) belonged to the East Tennessee, Virginia, and Georgia Railway, a predecessor of the Southern Railway. With the establishment of transfer yards at Spencer, North Carolina (1907), and Atlanta Inman Yard (1910), it became necessary to construct a transfer yard to serve Cincinnati, Louisville, St. Louis, and Memphis. A site was chosen in Knoxville for this facility, which would become known as John Sevier Yard. John Sevier, a pioneer settler and Revolutionary War hero, was the first governor of Tennessee.

Construction began on John Sevier Yard on July 24, 1924. The facilities would include a classification yard capable of handling 3,500 cars; engine handling facilities; a transfer station for handling less-than-carload freight moving through Knoxville; a refrigeration station for icing perishables; and pens where livestock could be fed, watered, and rested. The aerial view above shows John Sevier Yard looking toward the northeast with the Tennessee River on the right. (The Foundation Company.)

Two views of the 35-stall roundhouse at John Sevier Yard are shown on this page. The photograph above shows an aerial view of the roundhouse, while the one below shows a view looking northeast from the coaling station. Note the lack of engines and cars in these views, which were taken on October 25 and 26, 1925, immediately following the opening of the facility. (The Foundation Company.)

The view above shows the engine roundhouse looking north. To the left is the coaling tower. (The Foundation Company.)

This view of John Sevier Yard shows the coaling tower on the left with the roundhouse in the center and the classification yard on the right. (The Foundation Company.)

These two 1925 views of John Sevier Yard look west from the coaling station. On the previous page, one can see the coaling station from which these photographs were taken. The visible embankments give testimony to the impressive amount of grading that was necessary to create the space required for a rail yard. (The Foundation Company.)

In the early 1950s, John Sevier Yard was scheduled for a $2-million modernization. The Wright Construction Company of Columbus, Georgia, was awarded the contract, which was scheduled to be completed by January 1951. Torrential rains delayed the opening of the completed yard until May 1951. The yard remained in service throughout the construction process. When the modernization was completed, the eastbound and westbound receiving yards were consolidated, the classification yard was mechanized with push-button control switches and car retarders, and a new forwarding yard was constructed. Other modern improvements included floodlights, a loud speaker system, and pneumatic tubes to speed the handling of waybills (documents that covered the movement of each freight car). The photograph above shows the new car repair yard on the right and the engine house facilities in the background to the left. To the right, a cut of cars is being shoved up the hump to be classified.

In the photograph to the left, a two-unit yard switcher prepares to move a cut of cars up the hump with the use of a slug. A slug is a heavily weighted unit equipped with traction motors to provide extra power to yard diesels. The Slug, as it became known, was given on-the-job performance tests at John Sevier Yard.

The photograph on the right shows C. E. Galbraith, a car inspector, placing a Celotex wedge in the forward coupler as a car rolls up to the hump at John Sevier Yard. The use of the long pole allows the installation without the worker having to physically stand between the cars.

In the photograph above, a car goes through the initial 27-foot retarder. Flanges on the retarder will squeeze the car wheels to regulate its maximum speed to not more than four miles per hour. From here the cars will go through the main retarder which consists of three sections, each 44 feet long. As the cars continue their journey down the incline to the yard they will be directed to one of 46 classification tracks. There were a total of 16 retarders in the yard. During the time that John Sevier Yard was undergoing modernization, operations continued to take place despite the obvious construction of the control tower.

The photograph at right shows the car retarder classification system through the eyes of the controller. The initial retarder is controlled at the hump. The remaining retarders are controlled through this panel, which contains a schematic diagram of the classification yard. In the 1950s when this photograph was taken, the "magic of electronics" allowed for the making up of freight trains to speed them to far-away locations.

The photograph to the right is looking east down the hump toward the main retarder. The tower man estimates the retardation required by judging the speed through sight and sound. Radar control devices indicate the speed of the car when approaching the last retarder. All the components of the system were provided by the General Railway Signal Company.

This photograph was taken in July 1951 at John Sevier Yard and shows the completed main yard office. It is located at the crest of the hump. Serving as the nerve center of the yard, it houses the terminal trainmaster on the fifth floor and the scale clerk's office on the lower left.

This close-up photograph shows one of the 16 car retarders at John Sevier Yard. In the distance are the main yard tower and a diesel switcher that has just taken a cut of cars over the hump. There were seven diesel locomotives used in the yard, and each was equipped with a two-way radio that was set to one of three frequencies. The main radio station was located at the hump.

A cut of coal cars moves into the classification tracks at John Sevier Yard.

This is a close-up view of the car retarder, which, as its name implies, is a remote-controlled braking system that "retards" the speed of a car descending the hump. There needs to be sufficient speed to allow the car to enter the correct track, but the speed needs to be slow enough to prevent damage to the cars and their contents.

Another car goes into the classification yard.

The nerve center of yard operations is the yard offices on the hump. In these offices, a telegraph operator keeps posted on the arrival and departure of trains, a train clerk checks incoming trains, and a scale clerk weighs cars as they move across the hump. Waybills are collected for outgoing trains as shown in the photograph above. Part of the modernization of John Sevier Yard in 1951 was the installation of a pneumatic tube system, which connected the various yard offices to the main tower. This system consisted of seven lines with the longest being 9,200 feet. Hailed as a "state of the art system," the tubes carried waybills and other messages at the rate of 36 feet per second. The Southern Railway was also proud of the fact that these tubes were constructed of aluminum and would not require repainting. Other items in the photograph that are of interest are the rotary phone, the adding machine, the pencil sharpener, and the communications equipment being used by the employee on the right.

As the cars are moved from the receiving yard toward the hump, they pass between two car inspection pits constructed so that the inspector's eye level is the same as the top of the rail. The pits allow the most important parts of the car to be examined (above). If a defect is found in a car, it is immediately identified so that it can be diverted to the "bad order" track. The cars next pass a hot oil rack where men stationed on either side can raise the journal box lids and fill them with oil by means of a pressure gun connected to the heater and oil reserve tanks. This is a practice no longer seen, in that roller bearings have replaced the friction bearings that required regular lubrication (left).

The photograph above shows the automatic switching machine control panel in the hump conductor's office. The switches in the classification yard are controlled by the General Railway Signal automatic switching system. There are 46 push-button controls on this panel for the classification tracks. As a car approaches the hump, the conductor presses the control for the track where the car is to be routed. The classification tracks are capable of holding from 25 to 58 cars each. Pulling a classification track (making it unavailable for more cars) is accomplished by placing a metal yoke behind the numbered button on the panel.

Atlanta, Georgia, is shown in this aerial photograph taken in the 1950s. The two long rectangular buildings are the Southern Railway's office buildings. To the left of these buildings is the Atlanta Terminal Station. In 1972, the station was torn down and replaced by the Richard Russell Federal Office Building. In the foreground are the tracks over which such fine diesel-powered streamliners as the *Crescent*, the *Southerner*, and the *New Royal Palm* travel. The sheds alongside the two office buildings indicate that it is also the location of the Atlanta Freight Station. The tracks on the left side of the photograph lead to Inman Yard.

In the 1920s, Inman Yard, named for Civil War veteran and Atlanta businessman John H. Inman, was considered to be one of the most important facilities on the Southern Railway. At the time, the facilities in Atlanta included the Atlanta Terminal Station; the freight stations at Madison Avenue, Decatur Street, Simpson Street, and Roseland; and the main classification yard, transfer station, and icing station. The transfer station at Inman Yard was second in volume only to the one at Spencer, North Carolina. In the photograph above, two Mikados lead a freight train into Inman Yard. The lines of the Nashville, Chattanooga, and St. Louis Railway are on the left. The photograph below also shows steam power entering Inman Yard. (Top photograph: Frank E. Ardrey Jr.; bottom photograph: R. D. Sharpless, from the collection of Frank E. Ardrey Jr.)

Here are two photographs of Inman Yard taken sometime during the transition from steam to diesel locomotives (1941–1953). Both views were taken on the same day from the yardmaster's tower, with the interior photograph showing the yardmaster busy at work.

In 1955, it was announced that Inman Yard would undergo a $15-million expansion to include a new freight classification and forwarding yard. The photograph to the right was taken in January 1956 and shows the beginning phases of the construction. The yard would remain open, as shown in the photograph below of the passenger train making its uninterrupted journey.

The photographs on the next two pages show the construction of Inman Yard office, tower, and underpass. The photograph above was taken on July 10, 1956, while the photograph below was taken on October 29, 1956.

These photographs were taken on May 17, 1957, and show the tower nearing completion and rail leading to the classification yard being laid. In the photograph above, there is a view of the bridge. Rail traffic will go under the right side, while cars and other vehicles will travel on the left.

The bridge, which was under construction in the photograph on page 39, is shown here completed. An RS3 No. 2039 leaves the engine terminal and heads for Inman Yard. (Martin K. O'Toole.)

Some of the many workers in the Inman Yard tower are shown in this August 1957 photograph.

Work proceeds on the classification yard as shown in these May 1957 photographs. The view above shows the yard from the vantage point of the hump. In the photograph to the right, workers prepare one of the many lights that will be used to illuminate the yard.

With the classification yard complete, the Southern Railway goes about the business of making up trains.

A flat car loaded with lumber rolls down the hump toward the classification yard. Radar scanners, pictured in foreground, record the car's speed and transmit this information to the computer in the nearby retarder tower. Furnished with this and other knowledge about the car, the computer automatically controls the operation of the retarders to insure its safe passage into the classification yard.

These bridges carry Marietta Road over the south end of Inman Yard. Evidence of two public transit systems—repaving of the street following the removal of streetcar tracks and the dual overhead catenaries of the trolley bus system—can be seen in this 1956 photograph.

One of the most significant problems that railroads experienced in laying track was the use of the joints used to connect sections of rail. This problem was eliminated with the introduction of a continuous rail system known as ribbon rail. Southern Railway's Rail Welding and Track Assembly Facility were among the improvements made to Inman Yard. To the right is an aerial view of the facility, which produced sections of continuous rail over a quarter-mile in length.

This photograph of Inman Yard looks north. The classification yard can be seen near the top of the photograph in the center of the picture.

Two

Passenger Trains and Equipment

Technological change is generally evolutionary instead of revolutionary. This truth certainly applies to the changes in railway equipment designed to carry passengers. Over the years, passenger trains have evolved from the primitive to the elegant. In the 1830s, the South Carolina Canal and Railroad Company carried people in primitive, four-wheeled, wagon-type cars. By the time the Southern Railway stopped its passenger service, people were being transported in modern cars equipped with all the latest technology. Passenger cars saw an amazing metamorphosis from the 1830s to the 1850s, when the design changed from cars which resembled horse-drawn stage coaches to cars that looked like they belonged on the railroad. While the earliest cars were designed only to carry passengers in their seats, the modern cars provide passengers multiple opportunities for socialization, four-course meals, a comfortable night's rest, and the simple pleasure of watching the world go by from dome cars. On Christmas Day in 1830, the locomotive named the *Best Friend of Charleston* by the business people of Charleston, South Carolina (above), made its first trip pulling two small cars of passengers. It was so named because the leaders of the community saw the railroad as their best friend.

This 1892 photograph shows the open area at each end of the cars called a vestibule. This is the area where passengers would board and exit the cars. The raised center portion of the car is known as a clerestory roof. The development of this type of roof became widespread in the middle of the 19th century. Its purpose was to increase both light and ventilation in the years before air-conditioning.

It didn't take very long for railroad operators to learn what would be required of their equipment to safely carry passengers, and by the 1840s, the cars reflected those lessons. These cars, although from a later period, appear much like earlier cars with steps to facilitate boarding into an open vestibule and rudimentary protection from the weather.

A holdover from the pioneer era of railway passenger cars was their construction of wood despite predictably disastrous results in the event of a collision. As can be seen in this 1894 photograph of the wreck of Old 97, this type of construction offered precious little protection to its occupants. Another hazard was presented by the coal-fired heating stoves in the cars, which, in the event of a crash, frequently set fire to the wreckage.

In the later part of the 19th century, open vestibules began to disappear in favor of a closed type. During the early part of the 20th century, wooden passenger cars began to be replaced by cars that were constructed entirely of steel. This 1938 photograph, taken at Hawkinsville, Georgia, shows an interesting steel car with space for passengers and express shipments. The clerestory roof design is clearly visible. (Frank E. Ardrey Jr.)

This photograph was taken at the station in Augusta, Georgia, in the 1940s, and the train is about to depart for Branchville, South Carolina. A steel car is positioned behind the tender of locomotive No. 656—a U.S. railway mail car. These cars, which were once common, picked up and dropped off mail for each post office on the train's route. Postal clerks worked inside the cars sorting mail while the train hurried along. All of the cars in this view exhibit the clerestory type of roof.

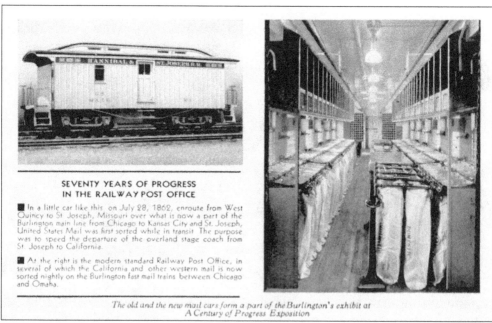

SEVENTY YEARS OF PROGRESS
IN THE RAILWAY POST OFFICE

■ In a little car like this on July 28, 1862, enroute from West Quincy to St. Joseph, Missouri over what is now a part of the Burlington main line from Chicago to Kansas City and St. Joseph, United States Mail was first sorted while in transit. The purpose was to speed the departure of the overland stage coach from St. Joseph to California.

■ At the right is the modern standard Railway Post Office, in several of which the California and other western mail is now sorted nightly on the Burlington fast mail trains between Chicago and Omaha.

The old and the new mail cars form a part of the Burlington's exhibit at A Century of Progress Exposition

This vintage postcard shows the earlier style of car with both the open vestibule and clerestory roof. It also gives us a glimpse of the interior of a railway post office car.

This 1951 photograph shows a train moving out of Inman Yard in Atlanta, Georgia, and illustrates the transition which took place during this time period. The *Sunnyland* from the Birmingham Division has in its contents a ten-section drawing room car with a two compartment sleeper. Notice that the cars have both clerestory and smooth rooftops. Interestingly, this train with cars of two different eras is being pulled by a modern diesel locomotive. (R. D. Sharpless, from the collection of Frank E. Ardrey Jr.)

Here are two interior views of coaches from two different eras. The photograph at the left shows the interior of a clerestory type roof. Notice the smaller windows that are a design holdover from the days before air-conditioning.

The photograph above shows a more modern interior with a smooth ceiling. The much larger windows were obviously intended never to be opened, a sure sign that the coach is air-conditioned.

In this mixed-era view, the *Southerner* is near Lenox Road in Atlanta, Georgia, with a steam locomotive pulling a train with a matched set of very modern rail cars, a type that could still be seen well into the late 20th century. (R. D. Sharpless, from the collection of Frank E. Ardrey Jr.)

By the 1930s, stainless steel was being successfully employed in passenger car construction and presented a modern appearance while lowering maintenance costs for the railroad. These cars present a remarkable contrast to the primitive cars of 100 years ago. (Industrial Photograph Company, Philadelphia, Pennsylvania.)

Dining cars were typically the most expensive cars to operate, but the passengers expected good food and service, and the railroads spared little expense in its preparation and presentation, as shown in this photograph. The amazing quality of dining car meals was made possible through the skill of railway chefs and the magic they performed within the cramped confines of dining car kitchens.

Just one more of the amenities of travel by rail—passengers socializing in a club-like atmosphere with a railroad hostess standing at the rear of the car ready to attend to the needs of her clientele—is pictured here. During the 1940s and 1950s, hundreds of women applied for the position of hostess on these trains. After meeting a very rigid set of entrance requirements, the hostesses began their duties, which were described as "making the passengers' trips as pleasant as possible."

In the photograph above, we see passengers enjoying the passing panorama from their vantage point in a dome car. Dome cars, known as vista domes, astra domes, blister domes, bubble domes, or glass tops, were very successful following their introduction in the mid-1940s.

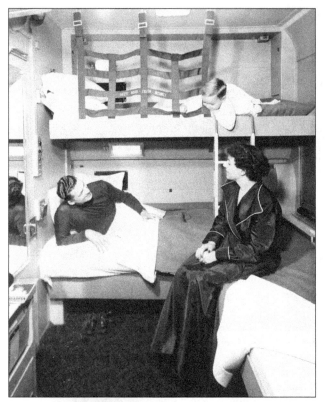

While there were some sleeping cars on the railroad prior to the 1850s, most railroads did not enter into this business until after the 1860s. The railroads realized that passengers had to be made as comfortable as possible, and the long-distance trips that were appearing all over the country necessitated the addition of the sleeping car to their fleets. Following World War II, the traveling public demanded more privacy while traveling. The photographs on this page illustrate a private room that has been converted into a bedroom for overnight travel.

Not every passenger train would include all types of passenger equipment. Only long-distance trains would require a full range of passenger services. In this photograph, a long distance train is shown with a round-end observation car bringing up the rear. (R. D. Sharpless, from the collection of Frank E. Ardrey Jr.)

Perhaps the best example of a modern, long-distance Southern Railway passenger train was the famous *Southern Crescent*. This was a train with both a remarkable history and longevity. Its roots go back into the 19th century with the railroad establishing service between Washington D.C., and New Orleans, Louisiana. The route of the train underwent changes and was given the name the *Crescent* in the 1920s. A second Southern Railway passenger train carried the name the *Southerner*, and in 1970, the two trains were combined into one with the name the *Southern Crescent*. In 1971, the nation's passenger trains were reorganized under Amtrak, and by 1979, the Southern Railway put the *Southern Crescent* into the Amtrak system. Today it is simply known as the *Crescent*. The photograph shows the northbound *Southern Crescent* north of Wells Viaduct near Toccoa, Georgia.

This sleeping car, part of a modern Amtrak long-distance train, was named "The W. Graham Claytor." Mr. Claytor was chairman and president of the Southern Railway and later held the same position with Amtrak. This superliner deluxe sleeper was the first such car placed into service by Amtrak in 1995. The photograph below was taken at the dedication of the car, and pictured, from left to right, are Bill Withuhn, Smithsonian Institution; Doug Varn, manager of Amtrak's Auto Train; and Jim Bistline, retired general counsel of Norfolk Southern Railway. They are touring a double-decker, sightseer lounge car. (Bill Shafer.)

In the 21st century, it is still possible to ride the *Crescent* as part of the Amtrak system that operates from New York City to New Orleans, Louisiana. The name *Crescent* was applied to the train in recognition of the crescent shape of the route that travels south from New York before gracefully swinging in a south-westerly direction to New Orleans. (Dick Hillman.)

At Washington's Union Station, a sleeping car attendant welcomes passengers aboard a modern Amtrak sleeping car. The train is the Amtrak *Crescent*. (C. Pat Cates.)

Three

THE SOUTHERN RAILWAY GOES TO WAR

The history of the United States Military Railway Service has its roots in the War Between the States, when Pres. Abraham Lincoln was authorized by Congress on January 31, 1862, "to take possession of, and place under military control, the country's telegraph lines and railroads." Thus was born the Military Railway Service. Following the Civil War, there was very little activity of the Military Railway Service. When the United States entered World War I, nine regiments of the Military Railway Service were authorized by General Order Number 61 of May 14, 1917. These units served in the southwest portion of France, and their duties included the hauling of men and supplies, placing cannons on railroad cars, and constructing railroad lines in various gauges. After World War I, it was determined that the regiment was not the best organizational unit for the Military Railway Service. The decision was made for individual railroads to sponsor a railway unit and to form a battalion of four companies. Company A would be trackmen and bridge carpenters; Company B was for the maintenance of equipment; Company C was for operations and a headquarters; and Service Company was formed for dispatchers, operators, and line repairmen as well as to supply housing, mess facilities, and supply operations. The officers for the battalion were commissioned according to the technical duties they performed on the railroad such as superintendent or engineer. Along the tracks of the Southern Railway at Hattiesburg, Mississippi, a sign appears announcing Fort Northeastern, a camp sponsored and named by the Southern Railway. Located near Camp Shelby, Fort Northeastern consisted of a private office car and 21 camp cars for use in connection with training of personnel. The Southern Railway also donated the flag pole shown in this picture.

In October 1929, Harry A. DeButts, vice president of operations of the Southern Railway, was asked by the War Department to organize a railway battalion. DeButts had served in the Marine Corps during World War I. The 594th Railway Operating Battalion was organized, and Mr. DeButts was made the first battalion commander. This was the parent organization of what was to become the 727th Railway Operating Battalion as preparations began for participation in World War II. The second battalion commander was Clark Hungerford, who was succeeded by Lt. Col. Fred W. Okie. The Southern Railway was the first railroad chosen for training of railway operating battalions. Hattiesburg, Mississippi, was chosen as the site for training as it was along the New Orleans and Northeastern Division of the Southern Railway. In this picture, taken in 1942, Col. (later brigadier general) Carl R. Gray Jr. (sixth from right) visits Fort Northeastern and Camp Shelby with Clark Hungerford, Southern Railway general manager of the Western Lines (fourth from right), and the officers of the 727th Railway Operating Battalion, including Lt. Col. Frederick William Okie (third from left). Colonel Gray was the general manager for the Military Railway Service.

On February 20, 1942, the
727th Railway Operating
Battalion, as later amended, was
ordered into military service.
The first group of officers
received their initial training
at Fort Wood, Missouri. The
following month, these officers
departed for Camp Shelby,
Mississippi. A meeting was held
at the high school auditorium in
Meridian, Mississippi, to discuss
the methods and purpose of
training of the members of the
Military Railway Service. The
pictures on this page are from
that meeting.

The Southern Railway furnished a private office car and 21 camp cars for use in the training of personnel. Pictured on this page are the officers of the 727th and Southern Railway officials meeting at Hattiesburg, Mississippi, in 1942. In the picture at left, Clark Hungerford, general manager of the Western Lines (center), is sharing a laugh with two unidentified companions.

In March 1942, the commanding officer of Camp Shelby welcomed the officers of the 727th Railway Operating Battalion. Unfortunately the camp for the new battalion had not been constructed. Construction began immediately, and it was decided to delay the activation of the enlisted men until April. The photograph above shows the barracks for Company A, while the bottom photograph shows the barracks for Company C.

Lt. Col. Frederick William Okie commanded the 727th Railway Operating Battalion from its activation until February 1945, when he was transferred to the command of the 704th Railway Grand Division. Okie, who was born in Dayton, Ohio, attended the Virginia Military Institute from 1925 to 1929. He entered the battalion as a first lieutenant around May 15, 1935, and was promoted to lieutenant colonel on August 15, 1941. Prior to that time, he was a superintendent of the Birmingham Division of the Southern Railway. Following World War II, he became president of a number of railroads, including the Bessemer and Lake Erie Railroad Company (1949); the Elgin, Joliet and Eastern Railway (1964); and the Duluth, Missabe and Iron Range Railway (1964). In 1968, he was elected president of the Pittsburgh and Conneaut Dock Company. (Bottom Photograph: National Archives and Records Administration.)

Southern Railway men in this picture of 727th officers taken at Camp Shelby in 1942 include (kneeling, second and third from the left) Lt. V. E. Williams and Lt. H. C. Mauney; (standing, first three on left) Lt. J. G. Beard, Capt. J. M. Boles, and Lt. Col. Okie. Capt. C. C. Mullen and J. R. Sterling are standing in the second row.

Lt. Vic Williams (shown on right) and an unidentified officer are seen outside the 727th Officer's Club.

This unidentified officer is photographed at the 727th Battalion Headquarters.

Remember that these men were soldier-railroaders. The first 400 men began receiving basic military training. In the picture above, which was taken in May 1942, members of Company A fall out for inspection with their weapons. Weapons training on the rifle range began in August of that same year. In the photograph below, members of the 727th Railway Operating Battalion attack the obstacle course.

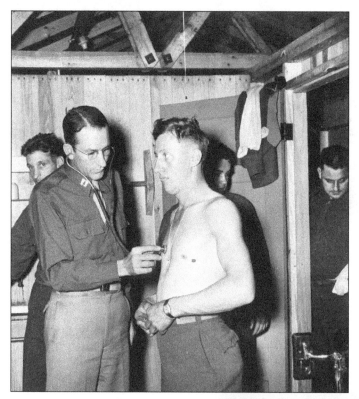

In the early stages of their training, there was no medical officer assigned to the 727th. Arrangements were made with the doctor at Post Dispensary 4 to provide necessary medical attention. Sgt. R. L. Stewart of the Headquarters and Service Company (H&S) was placed in charge, as he had considerable medical training. Qualified medical assistants were assigned as they joined, and thus the medical detachment of the 727th was formed. On June 24, 1942, 1st Lt. R. P. Osburn reported for duty and assumed command of the medical detachment. Capt. J. G. Peeler was assigned to the medical department on July 21.

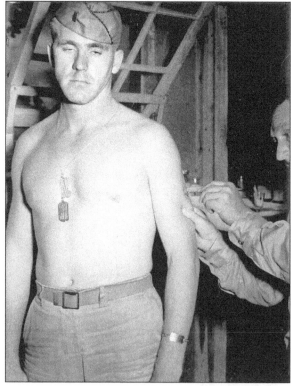

A soldier of the 727th Railway Operating Battalion undergoes one of the more unpleasant aspects of his medical procedures as can be seen by the expression on his face.

Troops of the 727th Railway Operating Battalion line up outside the post medical facility for physical examinations. The examinations were critical to the mission of the unit as well as part of the training of medical personnel.

On any railroad, communications are essential to safe and efficient operations, and troops of the 727th underwent rigorous training to insure those results.

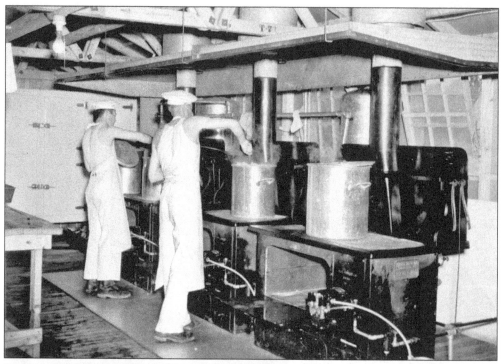

The maintenance of healthy, enthusiastic troops is dependent upon several factors, not the least of which is good, healthy food. Again, this translates to the need to train personnel to fulfill this part of the unit's mission. In these photographs, troops are seen learning how to prepare meals under military conditions and, in turn, provide meals for their fellow trainees.

In addition to the military training given to all the members of the 727th, the most important training, of course, was in the operation of railroads in the theater of war. While there was no precedent for this type of training, the Southern Railway based its training on two broad assumptions: first, that the battalion would be called on to operate an established railroad in some theater of operation that would employ every sort of temporary and make-shift facility; and second, that the greatest possible simulation of the conditions that might be encountered in such a theater of operations would provide the most effective training for the officers and men. To this end, the Southern Railway decided to give the 727th Railway Operating Battalion its own operation of the railway's line from Meridian, Mississippi, to New Orleans, Louisiana, with the understanding that the training could not interfere with the daily operation of the railroad. In the picture above, members of the 727th receive on-the-job instructions in repairing bridges on the New Orleans and Northeastern Division of the Southern Railway between Hattiesburg, Mississippi, and New Orleans, Louisiana.

While track maintenance is one of the less glamorous or exciting aspects of railroading, its importance cannot be over-emphasized. Experience taught military leaders that any railroad taken over by American troops under combat conditions would most likely have suffered catastrophic damage. Getting the track rebuilt quickly was the first objective of a military railroad unit, and training for this critical task was rigorous.

Technical training of the battalion began in April 1942. As the new men arrived, they were detailed as trackmen, bridge men, trainmen, engineers, shop men, operators, and dispatchers. The average railroad experience for the men of the 727th was 5.3 years. Men practicing their skills on tracks of the New Orleans and Northeastern Division of the Southern Railway can be seen here.

Railroad equipment is subjected to hard usage by the very nature of railroad operations, and the proactive maintenance of the equipment is essential to its survival. Teaching proper maintenance techniques was another important aspect of training a railway operating battalion. Soldier-railroaders working on locomotives are shown in these photographs.

Many of the recruits undergoing training at the Southern Railway facility at Meridian, Mississippi, were experienced railroaders, but everyone had to learn the new requirements of railroading under combat conditions. Here students quickly learn how to rebuild a damaged car and ready it for another load of military equipment.

Operating trains safely and efficiently requires great skill and knowledge. Because of the tremendous weight of rail equipment plus the heavy loads they transport, mishaps can have disastrous results. Efficiency, especially under combat conditions where fuel can be scarce, is another aspect of training. Getting every possible mile out of precious fuel and water is critical, and learning to do all of this was a big part of the training of personnel of the 727th Railway Operating Battalion.

It is a common assumption that a railroad engineer is in charge of his train, but that is not the case. With both passenger and freight trains, the conductor is assigned that responsibility. In the case of freight trains, the conductor's office was in the caboose. In these views, we see recruits undergoing the important training required to safely assume their responsibilities.

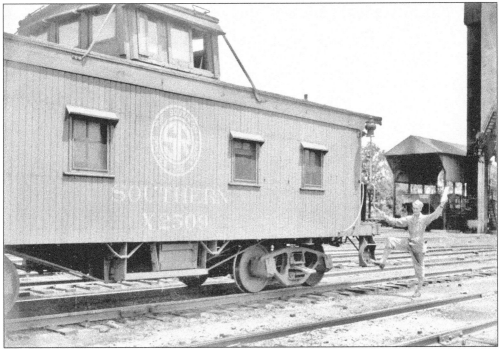

In August 1942, the 727th Railway Operating Battalion was notified to speed up all stages of their final training in preparation for embarkation in September. This would prove to be one of a number of false alerts for the battalion. On September 15, a formal inspection of all phases of military training was made by Brigadier General Gray, who reported that the training was completed "in a very satisfactory manner and that in most of the important subjects you have been generally rated excellent." In addition, Camp Shelby was inspected by President Roosevelt on September 29. In the photograph above, men of the 727th participate in one of the many parades that were held during the final weeks of their training.

The 727th was placed on alert on November 2 and again on November 9, 1942. On November 20, the battalion left on three trains, two from Camp Shelby and one from Key Field near Meridian, Mississippi. Southern Railway engine No. 727 handled the first train, manned by personnel of the battalion from Hattiesburg, Mississippi. Clark Hungerford, general manager, and Mr. Morris Stewart, superintendent of Motive Power, accompanied the train as far as Washington, D.C.

Its training completed, the 727th Railway Operating Battalion prepares to leave Hattiesburg, Mississippi, for the "theatre of operations" overseas. E. M. Tolleson, Southern Railway superintendent, tells Lt. Col. Fred W. Okie "good-bye and good luck."

Some of the men of the 727th Railway Operating Battalion, now a well-trained group of combat railroaders, gather at the Hattiesburg, Mississippi, depot ready to head off to war.

The 727th Railway Operating Battalion leaves Hattiesburg, Mississippi. The trains continued on to Fort Dix, New Jersey, where the men were moved into a tent camp in preparation for their overseas departure. In early December, the men were granted 24-hour leaves. By December 12, the battalion was loaded on three ships and left the port of New York. It was not until much later that they learned they would be landing in North Africa.

Men of the 727th Railway Operating Battalion ride a train heading for Fort Dix, New Jersey, on November 20, 1942. By December 26, 1942, the men would be docking at Mers El Kebir, near Oran, Algeria. By January 19, 1943, the 727th had assumed operation of the meter-gauge railroad lines in eastern Algeria and Tunisia. The Supreme Headquarters Allied Expeditionary Force (SHAEF) wanted to build up a large supply base in Tebessa, Algeria, in order to have the necessary forces to disrupt the line of the Germans and the Italians. The 727th was given the responsibility for transporting these supplies to Tebessa. The equipment was in very bad shape, and the 122-mile run took over 40 hours.

In early February 1943, Gen. Erwin Rommel, Germany's "Desert Fox," launched a major offensive toward Tebessa and the Kasserine Pass in North Africa. The 727th found itself working around the clock to remove equipment and supplies from the path of the German Army. By February 20, the American forces were routed from Kasserine Pass. General Rommel anticipated a counterattack by the Americans and halted his advance. This was a crucial mistake by the German commander and gave the Americans time to bring up reinforcements. With the supplies of his troops at a dangerously low level, Rommel made the decision to completely withdraw his army. As soon as the area was made safe by the Allies, the 727th unloaded the supply trains and returned to repairs and operation of the railroad. The picture above was taken of the Fifth U.S. Army, North Africa. "Will she make the grade?" query five GI passengers as the soldier-operated locomotive *Iron Bessie* strains and chugs up a long incline toward a mountain pass. This train is one of many that made runs throughout North Africa. (Photograph by Sgt. Joseph Hansen, Army Signal Corps.)

As the *North African Limited*—posted with the Fifth Army in North Africa—comes to a halt at a railroad junction, the soldier train crew takes time out for chow. An African locomotive of ancient vintage lumbers by pulling an army train in the opposite direction. (Photograph by Sgt. Joseph Hansen, Army Signal Corps.)

"Here goes my week's chocolate ration!" exclaims PFC James Gabazzo during a short stop at a railroad station in North Africa. He is surrounded by Arab children with hands extended who eagerly cluster around the amused soldiers. These men of the Fifth Army are passengers on a GI-operated train. Shown on the left, looking at the camera, is Pvt. Harold Zall. (Photograph by Sgt. Joseph Hansen, Army Signal Corps.)

An all-steel flat car is converted into an African Pullman by four tank men of the Fifth Army. Shelter halves and army blankets are the only materials necessary. Shown here, from left to right, are PFC James Gabazzo, Cpl. Jack Thompson, Cpl. Warren Fuerst, and Pvt. Harold Zall. (Photograph by Sgt. Joseph Hansen, Army Signal Corps.)

There are no worries about stuck windows for these tank men of the Fifth Army as they ride on an open-air African train. Cpl. Rhobidien Dyal gazes from the window of his half-track "Moonshine T." The three seated men are, from left to right, Cpl. Carrol Wetski, PFC Charles Fisher, and Sgt. H. L. Smith. (Photograph by Sgt. Joseph Hansen, Army Signal Corps.)

In the picture above, the *North African Limited* clicks smoothly across the flatlands of a grass-covered valley. In the distance lie the foothills of the mountains that the soldier-operated locomotive *Iron Bessie* must cross on her regular runs between North African cities, carrying troops and supplies for the Fifth Army. On June 21, 1943, the 727th was officially relieved from duties in North Africa and was sent to Sicily. It arrived in mid-July to support the Seventh Army under the command of Gen. George S. Patton, who conferred upon the battalion a commendation "for a job unparalleled in railroad history. The 727th landed its advance reconnaissance party as soon as a bridgehead had been established. Taking over an unfamiliar railroad system in a hostile country, it suffered under bombings and in the mine fields as did the combat troops, but nevertheless delivered the goods exactly as though it were running trains back in the states in peacetime." In November, the 727th was transferred to Italy, where it began the operation and maintenance of the Italian Railways in the southern part of the country around Salerno. (Photograph by Sgt. Joseph Hansen, Army Signal Corps.)

On January 17, 1944, the 727th was given charge of the port of Naples and its yards and rail installations. There were two raids on Naples by the Germans. One on March 15 resulted in two members of the 727th receiving Purple Hearts. Another raid was conducted on April 24, which resulted in one soldier receiving the Purple Heart. In the photograph to the left, two officers of the 727th inspect damage to the roundhouse as a result of one of these attacks.

In June 1944, the 727th Railway Operating Battalion was moved to Rome, where its duties included operating the west coast lines from the vicinity of Anzio. The photograph below shows the huge railway passenger terminal in Rome.

When railroading duties in Italy were concluded, the 727th Railway Operating Battalion was sent to southern France, where it arrived at the end of September. One of its major accomplishments was the construction of an 1,800-foot bridge over the Rhone River at Avignon. As the service of the 727th was drawing to a close in Europe, one of the most memorable moments for the battalion occurred in December at Lyon, France. The French rail system was known as the SNCF, and many of the employees of this line lost their lives during the war, leaving an incredible number of orphaned children. When Christmas arrived in 1944, the personnel of the 727th dealt with their own loneliness by putting together a Christmas party for the children of their lost brothers of the SNCF. The 727th, along with the 794th Military Police Battalion, purchased items from the PX (the post exchange) and saved materials from their own packages from home. Mess sergeants managed to scrounge up enough ingredients to produce prodigious amounts of hot chocolate and cookies. A large hall was sufficiently refurbished, and 1,800 children from throughout the SNCF Lyon District had a wonderful Christmas, which they would never forget. Pictured above is the cover from the program of that momentous day. (C. Pat Cates.)

FREEDOM CHRISTMAS PARTY
LYON - DECEMBER 24, 1944.

PROGRAM

ORCHESTRA AND CAROLS
ADVENTURES OF MICKEY MOUSE

-A CHRISTMAS STORY-

A ONE ACT COMEDY BY M. LEROUDIER
SANTA CLAUS - M. DUCRET
AN AMERICAN TOY- SGT. R. BEAUDRY
A DOLL — MLLE. NELLY
TWO CHILDREN-ARLETTE AND JEAN

ORCHESTRA AND CAROLS
CHILDREN' PARTY

THIS PARTY HAS BEEN
SPONSORED BY THE

727 TH.

RAILWAY OPERATING BATTALION

Shown are pages from the bilingual program showing both English and French languages.

ARBRE DE NOEL'
DE LA LIBERATION

LYON LE 24 DECEMBRE, 1944.

PROGRAMME

ORCHESTRE AVEC CHOEURS
LE PETIT MICHEY
DANS SES AVENTURES
(CINEMA)

-NOEL----- NOEL-

COMEDIE EN UN ACTE DE M. H. LEROUDIER
LE PERE NOEL — M. DUCRET
UN JOUJOU AMERICAIN
                - SERGENT R. BEAUDRY
UNE POUPEE — MLLE. NELLY
DEUX ENFANTS-ARLETTE ET JEAN
ORCHESTRE AVEC CHOEURS
GOUTER DES ENFANTS
CETTE SEANCE RECREATIVE EST
PLACEE SOUS LE PATRONAGE DU
727ᵉ BATAILLON DES CHEMINS
DE FER AMERICAINS

On April 18, 1945, the 727th Railway Operating Battalion left for Germany. Their mission was to work out from Mannheim through Heilbronn, Ludwigsburg, and Stuttgart in support of the Seventh Army. The war in Europe ended on May 7, 1945, and by September, most of the men of the 727th had returned to the states.

Four

WORKING ON
THE RAILROAD

A far-flung railway system requires an amazing array of skilled people. There are hundreds of vastly different jobs within a single railway company that must be carefully performed to permit the safe movement of both people and freight. These workers are deployed across the thousands of miles of a railway system, from executives in offices to men and women staffing the trains. There are crews of people making up trains in rail yards, crews repairing and upgrading the track, and shop personnel rebuilding locomotives and cars. In addition, there are inspectors checking trackside signals as well as looking for potential problems in the track. Dispatchers are located throughout the system that keep the rail traffic moving, and clerks handle the enormous amount of paperwork. This chapter will show some of these widely varying occupations and the dedicated people who perform their tasks so well. Here, conductors Williamson and Baker pose in front of a wood-bodied caboose on the Georgia, Southern, and Florida Divisions of the Southern Railway at Macon, Georgia, c. 1926. (John Baker Collection.)

This photograph includes employees that represent a variety of occupations. Shown, from left to right, are John Street, yard clerk; Ross Martin, yard clerk; Marvin Sparks, conductor; Sylvester Pounders, fireman; John Middleton, engineer; A. W. Spurgeon, switchman; and Hyman Pannell, switchman. The photograph was taken *c.* 1925 at Sheffield, Alabama. (Hyman Pannell Collection.)

Only two men in this distinguished group are identified. The year is 1908, and lined up in front of this four-wheel "bobber" caboose at Coster Shops in Knoxville, Tennessee, are at left, Charlie Watson, conductor, and right, Alex Richards, flagman.

Helping passengers make travel arrangements and issuing tickets required a large staff in the major cities across the Southern Railway system. Shown in this undated photograph at Birmingham, Alabama, are, from left to right, R. W. Plemmons, district passenger agent; M. F. Cumberland, chief clerk; Martha Hamilton, assistant city ticket agent; unidentified; L. E. Brice, city ticket agent; Esther Anderson, information and ticket clerk; P. A. Jenkins, division passenger agent; and S. H. Johnson, general passenger agent. Notice that the two ladies in the photograph are wearing uniforms very similar to those worn by onboard railway hostesses.

Infantile paralysis (polio) was a devastating illness across America during the 1940s and 1950s, and fund-raising to support treatment and a cure took on many forms. The railroads in the United States started a fund-raising drive called the "Hobo Basket." This basket circulated across rail systems collecting funds, and pictured here is the Southern Railway's Hobo Basket coming home to much fanfare, as it had raised over $11,000 in the fight against polio. The welcome home ceremony took place in October 1948 at the Thirty-Seventh Street Yard in Birmingham, Alabama. It included, from left to right, (first row) W. J. Culver, assistant repair foreman; Terry Tullos of Laurel, Mississippi, 1947's "poster boy;" Pres. Ernest E. Norris and Ralph Kinnane and Charles H. Pate, two of the basket's originators; (second row) Z. B. Greer, chairman of the Jefferson County March of Dimes; Kirby L. Stough, first conductor to handle the basket; H. Pat Russell, Alabama campaign director for the March of Dimes; Mrs. W. M. Hames; and Mrs. C. E. Tullos, mother of Terry.

It was not too long ago that a station agent and clerk worked in most railway stations as seen in this 1951 photograph of Hesler Lineburg, station agent at New Market, Virginia. Mr. Lineburg was a legendary instructor of new agents in the field of telegraphy. Before joining the Southern Railway, Mr. Lineburg was a radio operator with the merchant marines and served for nine years in the Washington, D.C., fire department.

The task of ensuring that the railroad was receiving payment for the transportation services it provided required many people. In many cases, that process began with the clerk at the local station. Shown here is Mrs. Ellen Powell at work in the station at Oak Ridge, Tennessee, in August 1950.

93

Princeton, Indiana
December 11, 1947

Mr. B. E. Young,
Ass't. to President, Southern R. R.
Washington, 13, D. C.

Dear Sir:

I have been requested to send to you the picture of
13 engineers, conductors all retired living at Princeton,
Indiana, giving the years of service and occupation with the
Southern Railroad.

Reading from left to right, front row:

Name	Position	Entered Service	Retired
Walter Skelton	Conductor	Aug. 16, 1897	Aug. 31, 1937
J. W. Hembree	Engineer	Aug. 2, 1909	Oct. 31, 1945
Gurnie Malone	Fireman	Aug. 4, 1903	Mar. 30, 1943
John L. Bennet	Engineer	May 1, 1893	July 1, 1937
G. W. Shircliff	Engineer	Aug. 8, 1903	Jan. 8, 1945
Thomas F. Finney	Engineer	Sept. 8, 1898	Aug. 1, 1937
W. A. Harder	Conductor	Mar. 17, 1910	June 14, 1938
William V. Miller	Engineer	Aug. 8, 1885 (L.E. & St. L. Railroad)	Aug. 1, 1937

Back row left to right:

Charles E. Rush	Conductor & Trainmaster	Aug. 6, 1898	Sept. 1, 1939
V. N. Camden	Yardmaster	Jan. 12, 1905	Feb. 1, 1940
A. F. Schmicker	Conductor	Oct. 5, 1905	Dec. 1, 1944
Clyde Woods	Engineer	Feb. 22, 1901	Mar. 31, 1945
William H. Morris	Conductor	Jan. 1, 1900	Nov. 16, 1935

Yours truly,

Ralph C. Cato

Ralph C. Cato
Occupation, Diesel Trainman
St. Louis Division

The service of these distinguished gentlemen is summarized at left. Pictured below from left to right are (first row) Walter Skelton, Bill Hembree, Gurnie Malone, John L. Bennett, G. W. Shircliff, Tom Finney, W. A. Harder, and Billie Miller; (second row) Charles E. Rush, V. N. Camden, Al Schmicker, Clyde Woods, and William Morris.

In this mid-1940s photograph, two men with high-ranking positions with the Southern Railway are having a meeting at Pratt Yard in Birmingham, Alabama. Shown are David C. Ferguson, superintendent terminals (left) and R. W. Hutto, general yardmaster (right).

Also at Pratt Yard, G. T. Haley utilizes communication equipment to talk to the tower that controls the switching of cars.

Spencer Shops was an enormous Southern Railway repair facility at Spencer, North Carolina. The huge roundhouse located within that complex was named for Bob Julian, a highly regarded roundhouse foreman. In this 1947 photograph, Mr. Julian stands in front of locomotive No. 4836, a 2-8-2 steam engine built in 1923 and scrapped in 1952. (David Driscoll.)

Mr. V. R. Weant stands in front of steam locomotive No. 1210 in this September 1946 photograph taken in the roundhouse at Spencer Shops. No. 1210, a 4-6-2, was built in 1904 and retired in 1951. (David Driscoll.)

Just like automobiles on a highway, trains have traffic control signals that must be obeyed. These signals require diligent inspection and maintenance. Shown here is L. E. Walke, a signal department supervisor, standing in front of one of these important signals on the Washington Division of the Southern Railway.

It is vitally important to train new employees so they are capable of both utilizing and maintaining critical elements in the safe operation of a railroad, such as the trackside signal system. This photograph was taken at the railroads training center in McDonough, Georgia.

Track maintenance and repair has always been a very labor-intensive job. It takes a great deal of manpower, skill, and equipment to get the job done properly and quickly. In this photograph, members of a crew are replacing sections of 131-pound rail. This term means that a three-foot section of this rail will weigh 131 pounds.

When first looking at this picture, one might think it is the kitchen of a dining car preparing meals for its passengers. This crew is actually in a camp car kitchen, and they're preparing food for a gang of hungry workers. The man in the foreground is track engineer Norman Cary.

It was previously mentioned that track repair needed to be completed quickly so as not to impede the movement of trains. In this photograph, track work has stopped and equipment moved aside in order for a passenger train to keep its schedule.

One of the more legendary occupations within the track maintenance field was that of the gandy dancer. These men worked as a well-coordinated team and were extremely proficient in aligning track so as to be straight as an arrow. In this photograph, the man in the foreground is looking through a surveying transit and directing the movement of the track until it is perfectly aligned.

Many people believe that the engineer is the person in charge of the train, but such is not the case. The conductor is the boss, and on a passenger train one of his important tasks is insuring that all of the passengers have the proper ticket. In this photograph, a conductor is shown examining tickets. Once he has verified that all is in proper order, he punches the ticket. These punches were equipped with an amazing variety of dies that made the punched hole identifiable as to the conductor who punched the ticket.

People who live near the rail line often become familiar to train crews and will often build a special friendship. One colorful example of this occurred near Rader, Tennessee, where train crews had the habit of dropping off newspapers and magazines for a rural family. The family's delivery system was Rex, the dog. As soon as Rex heard the approaching train, he dashed trackside and waited for the packages. Upon retrieval, Rex dutifully made the delivery to the family home. During the Christmas season in 1949, one train crew decided to make a very brief stop to meet their friend Rex and bring him a couple of gifts. In this photograph, Rex, the "Special Delivery Dog at Rader, Tennessee," had a surprise Christmas party when the *Tennessean* stopped at the farm of J. R. Myers. Shown from left to right are Charles Earnest, engineer; R. D. Merrell, fireman; A. B. Brackett, conductor; Mildred Edmunds, hostess; and Rex.

Shown in this 1930s photograph are the Southern Rails, the Southern Railway baseball team at Sheffield, Alabama, where they just concluded a successful season, winning 22 of their 31 games. According to the *Tri Cities Daily*, Sheffield's newspaper, "the Rails played better than average ball and their games attracted the largest crowds ever. They won the district championship indisputably by winning every series played against the teams in the immediate district." The players are, from left to right, (first row) L. Wilson, section laborer; M. Smith, trucker; G. W. Williams, clerk; Luke Hendricks, baggage clerk; and O. H. Hutto, clerk signal department; (second row) Mr. Arthur, clerk; Mose Chaffin, yard clerk; C. E. Manush, air brake foreman; (third row) L. M. Stevenson, clerk signal department and team manager; Charles White, storehouse department; Bill Crittenden, clerk; Clyde Lamb, building and bridge laborer; G. W. Johnson, trucker; and L. Battle, clerk.

Five

STEAM TRAINS ON THE SOUTHERN RAILWAY

Any discussion centering on the Southern Railway (and later the Norfolk Southern Railway) Steam Excursion Program will inevitably include references to three men: Graham Claytor, chairman and president, who made it possible; Jim Bistline, general counsel who ran the operation; and Bill Purdie, master mechanic, steam, who kept the machinery running. Sadly this work is too late to include interviews with Graham Claytor, but it is not too late to include the recollections of Jim Bistline and Jim Purdie, both at the brink of their 90th birthdays and both full of wonderful memories of the exciting and fulfilling years of steam excursions. The grand finale of the 25th Anniversary Celebration of Southern Railway/Norfolk Southern's Steam Excursion Program on November 3, 1991, featured a triple-headed 4501, 611, and 1218 from Chattanooga. The train originated at the rear of the Chattanooga Choo Choo and ran triple headed to Ooltewah, Tennessee, where the train was split into two sections. The 611 and 1218 double headed to Atlanta, Georgia, while the 4501 headed north to Cleveland, Tennessee. The Atlanta section terminated at the Southern Railway's Peachtree Station so passengers could connect with Amtrak's northbound *Crescent*. The Cleveland section was turned on a wye in Cleveland and returned via the same routing to Chattanooga. The photograph above was taken at Cohutta, Georgia, after the train was split at Ooltewah, Tennessee. (Alex Mayes.)

On Friday, January 28, 2005, authors Dick Hillman and Pat Cates interviewed Jim Bistline at his home, which was filled with a tremendous collection of railroad memorabilia. Mr. Bistline entertained the two authors for hours with the memories of his life and career with the railroad. "One of my more memorable early train rides," Jim advised, "occurred in 1921 when I was six years old. I had a wreck with my tricycle that resulted in the near removal of my nose. My father knew the agent at the Pennsylvania Railroad depot in Newport, Pennsylvania, and he hustled me down there. The agent was able to flag down the *Limited* (which was most definitely not scheduled to stop in the small town), and I was rushed to a hospital in Harrisburg where they re-attached my nose." Jim Bistline (left) poses in his study with Southern Museum of Civil War and Locomotive History employees Dick Hillman and C. Pat Cates. (George W. Hamlin.)

Jim's family always seemed to live near railroads, which became an early source of entertainment for him. In 1933, he graduated first in his class from high school in Cumberland, Maryland, and went to Duke University, where he once again graduated first in his class. After he received his law degree from Columbia Law School, he went to work for a Wall Street law firm until called into military service in 1942. Jim spent five years with the Judge Advocate General's Staff participating in the Nuremburg trials and successfully prosecuting some American thieves accused of stealing the Hess family jewels. Jim Bistline (left) appears on the cover of *TIES* Magazine (July–August 1981) as a conductor in the British Broadcasting Company's production of *Lady Astor*. Bistline served as a technical advisor for the nine-part television series. Shown in the center is British star Lisa Harrow, who portrayed Lady Astor. Edmond Bennett is on the right. (*TIES* Magazine.)

Upon returning to civilian life and in response to his deep love of the railroad industry, Jim accepted a position as an attorney with the Southern Railway in 1948. In 1964, he became general counsel, a senior position in the law department of the railway. At that time, Graham Claytor (shown on the right in the above photograph) was vice-president under Pres. D. W. Brosnan. "Bill" Brosnan (shown on the left) was not a steam fan, yet Claytor and Bistline were able to create a fledgling steam excursion program during the Brosnan regime. It needs to be added here that steam excursions already existed prior to the Southern Railway organizing their own program. One of these pre-existing excursion programs was operated by the Atlanta Chapter of the National Railway Historical Society (NRHS).

In the mid-1960s, the Atlanta Chapter was given permission to operate their steam-powered *Georgia Peach Special* excursion train out of Atlanta over Southern Railway lines. These trains were pulled by former Savannah and Atlanta Railway steam locomotive No. 750, and the engine was accompanied by a Southern Railway machinist who was charged with keeping the ancient machine running. The machinist assigned to this task was William J. (Bill) Purdie Jr. Bill was interviewed on February 17, 2005, at his home in Alpharetta, Georgia. He told of his first encounter with the man who was to make a profound impact on his life—Graham Claytor. This encounter occurred in the most unlikely place—on the tender of locomotive No. 750. With the cab crowded with guests, Bill had to ride on the tender. Claytor observed Purdie on the tender and inquired if he could join him for the ride. Claytor and Purdie rode the entire length of the trip on the tender, and thus began a long, fruitful friendship. The trio of Graham Claytor, Jim Bistline, and Bill Purdie, who were to run the Southern Railway's steam excursion program, was thus born. The photograph above shows Savannah and Atlanta Railway's No. 750 at Union Point, Georgia, on a NRHS trip on May 25, 1963. (W. F. Beckum, from the collection of Frank E. Ardrey Jr.)

Master Mechanic Bill Purdie was frequently photographed during his long career with the Southern Railway. He will be quick to point out, however, that this is his favorite photograph. Taken on November 28, 1972, at a NRHS Atlanta Chapter Atlanta-to-Birmingham trip, the photograph shows Bill talking with a kindergartner who is in awe at being in the presence of such a great man. (Photograph copyright 2005, *The Birmingham News*. Reprinted with permission.)

Jim Bistline tells the following story about the beginning of Southern Railway's steam program: "The National Railway Historical Society's National Convention of 1966 was in Richmond, Virginia, and locomotive No. 4501 was to be featured. We needed to move the engine from Chattanooga, Tennessee, to Richmond and routed it through Asheville, North Carolina, near where Bill Brosnan had his summer home. We arranged for Bill and a large crowd to be on hand to see No. 4501 come through knowing that Bill would be impressed by the scene. It worked, and Brosnan gave the go-ahead to the steam excursion program that Graham Claytor was then able to announce at the Richmond Convention." In the photograph above, locomotive No. 4501 dramatically departs the Richmond, Fredericksburg and Potomac Railroad's Broad Street Station, Richmond, Virginia, at 9:30 a.m. on September 25, 1966, for a northbound run over the "Capitol Cities Route" to Union Station. (W. E. Griffin Jr.)

Not only was Mr. Brosnan duly impressed by the passing of locomotive No. 4501, but so were the news reporters covering the story. One writer described the locomotive's passing as a spectacle "of furious whistle blasts and cinder fallout. It was grand, dirty, loud, sometimes fast, once frustrating, predictably memorable, and ultimately successful. No. 4501, restored to Southern Railway décor by Paul Merriman proved a willing if somewhat lame iron horse. Her valve timing was badly off . . . but she was wonderfully audible and given to bursts of up to 50 mph-plus . . . the engine consumed only 8 of the 18 tons of coal aboard because at least a quarter of the fuel barely grazed the fire, rifled through the tubes and up the stack, then reminded all the riders why there was so much excitement about the introduction of air-conditioning years ago, . . . Extra 4501 South impressed people, not to mention horses, cows, dogs and one mule. The animals stared, and then bolted. The people, riders or onlookers, were entranced. And big, bluff Road Foreman of Engines Walter Dove was at the throttle . . . thundering past Citico Yard with the whistle cord tied down, putting on the dog for all the admiring engine crews and yard clerks and switchmen that we swept past, giving the Mike her head. He hadn't lost his touch." In the photograph above, locomotive No. 4501 is shown on the track at the Richmond, Fredericksburg and Potomac Railroad's Bryan Park Terminal in Richmond, Virginia. (W. E. Griffin Jr.)

In 1967, Claytor became president of the Southern Railway and organized a formal steam excursion program. Jim Bistline was appointed to run this program in addition to his duties as general counsel. "I continued in both roles until 1974 when I became assistant to the president, handling the steam program along with my other duties." In the photograph to the right, Graham Claytor looks over a possible candidate for his steam excursion program.

Ex-East Tennessee and Western North Caroline Railroad locomotive No. 722 pulls an excursion train at Heflin, Alabama. (O. W. Kimsey, from the collection of Frank E. Ardrey Jr.)

The backdrop for this photograph is the old depot at Rural Retreat, Virginia, the location of a famous photograph taken by the late O. Winston Link. (Ron Flanary.)

The 4501, on the Atlanta-to-Birmingham ferry trip, crosses the Coosa River at Riverside, Alabama, on July 15, 1967. (Don Phillips.)

Southern Railway's No. 4501 meets northbound train No. 154 near Brice, Georgia, in June 1967. Brice is on the rail line from Atlanta to Rome, Georgia.

Locomotive No. 4501 was built in 1911 by the Baldwin Locomotive Works and purchased by the Southern Railway that same year. In 1948, it was sold to the Kentucky and Tennessee Railway, headquartered in Stearns, Kentucky. The Kentucky and Tennessee Railway sold the locomotive to Paul Merriman in 1963. Merriman was one of the founders of the Tennessee Valley Railroad Museum in Chattanooga, Tennessee, which currently owns the locomotive. The photograph above shows the 4501 at the Bryan Park Terminal in Richmond, Virginia, where she was brought in for repairs to her pony-truck wheels in 1966. (W. E. Griffin Jr.)

An interesting piece of trivia with the Southern Railway steam excursion program is that two different locomotives numbered 610 were utilized. In the mid-1970s, it became clear that larger locomotives capable of pulling larger trains would be required. In 1977, they leased ex-Texas and Pacific No. 610 from the 610 Foundation of Texas and used it frequently for several years. According to Bill Purdie, No. 610 could "move Stone Mountain."

In 1990, locomotive No. 1218 was laid up for repairs. Ex-U.S. Army locomotive No. 610, owned by the Tennessee Valley Railroad Museum (TVRM), was used as a substitute on the Huntsville to Chattanooga trip. Later it took the place of an ailing No. 4501 on trips between Huntsville and Knoxville and again in 1993 for a trip to Sandersville, Georgia. In the above photograph, TVRM No. 610 is crossing the Tennessee River east of Bridgeport, Alabama, in August 1990. Notice the Norfolk Southern Railway diesel behind No. 610. (Dick Hillman.)

Ex-Savannah and Atlanta Railway No. 750 runs the *Boy Scout Special* at Chamblee, Georgia, around July 1974. (Bill Schafer.)

Savannah and Atlanta Railway No. 750 and two FP7s head back to Richmond on one of the many Old Dominion Chapter NRHS trips between Richmond and Keysville for the latter's "Dixie Days" Festival. The train is seen crossing U.S. Highway 460 south of Jetersville, Virginia, on July 23, 1983. (Jim King.)

On a rainy Saturday, locomotives No. 722 and No. 750 were hauling a heavy train of excursion passengers from Alexandria to Strasburg, Virginia. At The Plains, Virginia, a combination of wet rails and damp sand in the locomotives' sanding equipment prevented the crew from getting the train underway. In the photograph at the right, taken on October 2, 1971, an unidentified crewman is seen spreading sand onto the tracks from a borrowed cookie tin. In the photograph below, we see Bill Purdie (top, left) and below him Walter Schweinebraten. On the right running board is Albert Dinkins, general road foreman of engines. Later two diesel locomotives arrived to get the train underway.

The American Freedom Train traveled throughout the United States as a part of the Nation's Bicentennial, and the locomotive assigned to this duty, ex-Southern Pacific No. 4449, was temporarily stored at Southern Railway's Birmingham, Alabama, shops. In August 1976, the engine was to move to Washington, D.C., to be reunited with her train. As *Trains Magazine* editor David Morgan stated, "Moving the engine by itself to Washington would have been unthinkable to Graham Claytor." As a result, the Southern Railway sponsored an Atlanta-Alexandria, Virginia, one-way trip behind locomotive No. 4449 that was enjoyed by 2,000 passengers and countless spectators. (Giles Y. Mebane, M.D.)

Graham Claytor (at right) left the Southern Railway in 1976 and was followed by Stane Crane, who, according to Jim Bistline, "tolerated the [steam] program." Harold Hall became president in 1979, and while he was more negative about the program, he soon became aware of the fact that the next chairman would be Bob Claytor, Graham Claytor's brother. Harold Hall knew that discontinuing the steam program would be ill-advised. When Bob Claytor (at left) became chairman, Hall continued as president. "Bob Claytor was, of course, very committed to the steam excursion program, and it flourished under his watch." Jim Bistline continued as manager of the steam program until his retirement in 1986.

Ex-Nickel Plate Railroad engine No. 765 was used for a short time and is seen here on October 31, 1982, on an Atlanta-to-Toccoa trip. (Jim King.)

Savannah and Atlanta Railway No. 750 and a pair of Southern FP7s head up the *Skyline Limited* excursion from Alexandria to Front Royal, Virginia, on Southern's Manassas Gap Branch on July 2, 1983. In the photograph, the train is passing through Delaplane, Virginia, en route to Front Royal. (Alex Mayes.)

On the right is another photograph of the *Skyline Limited* proceeding west to Front Royal taken near Markham, Virginia. The trip was sponsored by the Washington, D.C., and Potomac Chapters of the NRHS and the Chesapeake Division of the Railroad Enthusiasts. (Alex Mayes.)

The Old Dominion Chapter (ODC) of the NRHS sponsored the *Richmond Special* from Alexandria to Richmond, Virginia, on July 17, 1983. This trip marked the Chapter's 150th rail excursion. In this photograph, Jim Bistline (shown third from left) is helping the ODC Chapter members and Norfolk Southern Railway steam program officials celebrate the milestone following the excursion's arrival at the Richmond Amtrak Station. (W. E. Griffin Jr.)

Savannah and Atlanta Railway's No. 750 and Southern FP7s No. 6141 and 6143 (also seen on page 4) head up the Old Dominion Chapter NRHS *Dixie Limited* on Southern's line between Richmond and Keysville, Virginia, on July 23, 1983. The train is shown here near Burkeville, Virginia. The trip was one of five featured during the 1983 NRHS Convention held in Richmond and sponsored by the Old Dominion Chapter of the NRHS. Five hundred eighty passengers enjoyed this excursion. (Alex Mayes.)

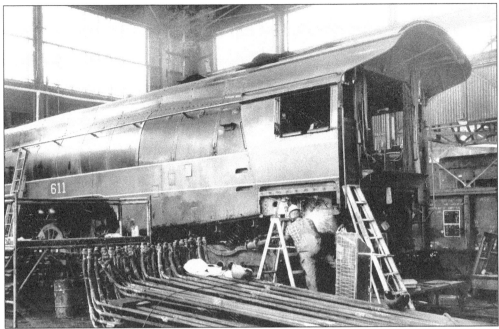

With Bob Claytor's arrival as chairman of the board in 1982, the steam program once again became a priority. One of Mr. Claytor's first decisions was to get Norfolk and Western locomotive No. 611 (upper photograph) up and running so that it could be added to the excursion fleet. This was completed by the fall of 1982. Five years later, locomotive No. 1218 (lower photograph) joined No. 611 as the pride of the Norfolk Southern steam excursion fleet. Both of these locomotives were originally built in the company shops of the Norfolk and Western Railway in Roanoke, Virginia. Both engines were removed from display and ferried to the Norfolk Southern shops in Birmingham, Alabama, where they were restored for steam excursion service.

The photograph above appears to be an optical illusion. Actually the locomotive is articulated; in other words, it is constructed to allow better tracking through curves.

Norfolk and Western Railway No. 1218, northbound on the Norfolk Southern Railway main line, crosses the Tye River north of Monroe, Virginia, on May 14, 1988, on the final leg of the Alexandria to Lynchburg, Virginia, excursion. (Alex Mayes.)

Locomotive No. 1218, pulling a 21-car train, enters a curve west of Jarrett Tunnel on the Norfolk Southern's Blue Ridge grade between Old Fort and Ridgecrest, North Carolina, on October 22, 1989. (Jim King.)

In his interview, Bill Purdie mentioned a number of locomotives that he came to know and love. One of his most pleasant memories centered around one of the more modern, mainline engines that he first encountered—ex-Canadian Pacific Royal Hudson No. 2839. In 1979, he headed south with the engine and happily proclaimed, "Now I've got an engine that will outrun the rail fans." In the photograph above, the 1980 excursion season saw the very different face and colors of Canadian-Pacific No. 2839 as it traveled over Southern Railway rails into Monroe, Virginia. (Curt Tillotson Jr.)

En route home from an Alexandria-to-Charlottesville, Virginia, excursion, locomotive No. 611 is northbound near Culpepper, Virginia. (Alex Mayes.)

The photograph above shows locomotive No. 1218 with an excursion train traveling across the massive James River Bridge north of Lynchburg, Virginia, on May 14, 1988. (Alex Mayes)

A pair of unlikely stable mates rest at Norfolk Southern's Armour Yard at Atlanta, Georgia. The date is October 30, 1987, and on the following day, locomotive No. 1218 will pull the Atlanta Chapter of the NRHS "Autumn Leaves" trip to Toccoa, Georgia. (Dick Hillman.)

The end of the Southern Railway/Norfolk Southern Steam Excursion Program was officially announced on October 28, 1994. The announcement resulted in a near avalanche of protest from rail fans throughout the United States. Railway officials revealed that some 2,000 to 3,000 letters of protest were received but to no avail. Letters from stockholders, civic leaders, children, and others pleaded with the company not to discontinue the program, and many of these letters were truly poignant. One 13-year-old wrote to the chairman of Norfolk Southern politely asking that the company not proceed with the termination and closed his request with a poem he had written, with the last verse quoted here: "We will have our memories for souvenirs, As well as our disappointment and tears. To keep 611 running would not be a mistake, but it would make many happy and end this heartache." The photograph above shows No. 611 crossing the Yadkin River in North Carolina. (Alex Mayes.)

In concluding his discussion on the excursion program, Jim Bistline told the authors that, "I'm often asked about the decision to terminate the steam program. Simply put, when the end of the program was announced in October 1994 it saddened me because it could have been handled better. The program really did become too large to be incorporated into a busy railroad, and the heavy workload created by the excursions was being added to the already heavy workloads of the operating department personnel. In my opinion a better solution would have been to follow the example of the Union Pacific Railroad where they operate eight or ten excursions a year." The final Norfolk Southern steam-powered excursion ran between Birmingham, Alabama, and Chattanooga, Tennessee, on December 3, 1994. Locomotives No. 611 and No. 1218, the last company-owned steam locomotives, were returned to Roanoke, Virginia, where they are now on display in the Virginia Transportation Museum. (Robert Lyndall.)

ACKNOWLEDGMENTS

The authors are grateful to the following persons for their contributions:

Nancy L. Bartol, librarian, Kalmbach Publishing Company, Milwaukee, Wisconsin
Sara Brabender, intern, Kennesaw Mountain High School, Kennesaw, Georgia
Jim Bistline, Norfolk Southern Corporation, retired
Virginia K. Cochenour, senior manager personnel administration, Transtar, Inc., Pittsburgh
Dr. Jeffrey A. Drobney, executive director, Southern Museum of Civil War and Locomotive History
George Eichelberger, director technical and marking services, T-Cubed, a subsidiary of Norfolk Southern Corporation
George W. Hamlin, director, MergeGlobal, Inc., Arlington, Virgina
Mary Beth Luczak, Simmons-Boardman Publishing Corporation, New York
Robert Lyndall, professional photographer, Roanoke, Virginia
Frederick W. Okie Jr., Pittsburgh
Martin K. O'Toole, attorney at law, Marietta, Georgia
William J. Purdie, master mechanic, steam, Southern Railway, retired
Cashin Riddell, intern, Kennesaw Mountain High School, Kennesaw, Georgia
David Russell, Russell Image Processing, Atlanta
Bill Schafer, director corporate affairs, Norfolk Southern Corporation
Linda Stafford, *The Birmingham News*

BIBLIOGRAPHY

Afrikakorps. Alexandria, VA: Time-Life Books, 1990

Coniglio, John William. *Steam in the Valley*. Hixson, TN: 1998.

Davis, Burke. *The Southern Railway, Road of the Innovators*. Chapel Hill, NC: University of North Carolina Press, 1985.

Galloway, Duane and Jim Wrinn. *Southern Railway's Spencer Shops 1896–1996*. Lynchburg, VA: TLC Publishing, 1996.

Gray, Carl R. *Railroading in Eighteen Countries, The Story of American Railroad Men Serving in the Military Railway Service 1862–1953*. New York: Charles Scribner's Sons, 1955.

Martin, Jean. *Mule to Marta, Volume II, 1902–1950*. Atlanta: Atlanta Historical Society, 1977.

Okie, Lt. Col. Fred W., Lt. Col. John M. Budd. *The 727th Railway Operating Battalion in World War II*. New York: Simmons-Boardman Publishing, 1948.

Prince, Richard Prince. *Southern Railway Steam Locomotives and Boats*. Millard, NE: 1970.

Schafer, Bill, ed. *Weekend Steam*. Spencer, NC: Southern Railway Historical Society, 1992.

The Southern Front. Alexandria, VA: Time-Life Books, 1991.

Southern News Bulletin. November 1925

Southern New Bulletin. December 1925

Southern News Bulletin. January 1928

"The Southern's John Sevier Yard—An Integrated Freight Terminal." *Railway Age*. August 6, 1951: pp 46–51.

"The Southern's John Sevier Yard—How Its Modern Facilities Speed Classification," *Railway Age*. August 6, 1951: pp. 52–56.

Webb, William. *The Story of the Southern Railway System, An Illustrated History*. Erin, Ontario: The Boston Mills Press, 1986.

White, John H. *The American Railroad Passenger Car*. Baltimore: The John Hopkins University Press, 1978.

Ziel, Ron, and Mike Eagleson. *Southern Steam Specials*. Bloomfield, NJ: 1970.